I

Walt Whitman's

am with

Leaves of Grass

YOU

1855–2005

I

Walt Whitman's

am with

Leaves of Grass

YOU

1855–2005

Isaac Gewirtz

The New York Public Library

2005 • New York

Published for the exhibition *"I Am with You": Walt Whitman's* Leaves of Grass *(1855–2005)*
presented at The New York Public Library
Humanities and Social Sciences Library
Sue and Edgar Wachenheim III Gallery
September 9, 2005–January 8, 2006

Support for The New York Public Library's Exhibitions Program has been provided by
Pinewood Foundation and by Sue and Edgar Wachenheim III.

This publication is made possible by the Henry W. and Albert A. Berg Collection of
English and American Literature.

Library of Congress Cataloging-in-Publication
Data

Gewirtz, Isaac.
   I am with you: Walt Whitman's Leaves of
grass (1855–2005) / Isaac Gewirtz.
      p. cm.
   "Published for the exhibition presented at the
New York Public Library, Humanities and Social
Sciences Library, Sue and Edgar Wachenheim III
Gallery, September 9, 2005–January 8, 2006."
   Includes bibliographical references.
   ISBN 0-87104-456-0 (pbk. : acid-free paper)
   1. Whitman, Walt, 1819–1892. Leaves of grass—
Exhibitions. I. New York Public Library.
Humanities and Social Sciences Library. II. Title.
   PS3238.G48 2005
   811'.3-dc22

                      2005022653

Karen Van Westering, Manager, NYPL
   Publications
Barbara Bergeron, Editor

Designed by Catherine Harvey
Cover design by Suzanne Doig

The New York Public Library
www.nypl.org

CONTENTS

6   PREFACE

10   "I AM WITH [SOME OF] YOU"

47   CHECKLIST OF THE EXHIBITION

51   SELECTED BIBLIOGRAPHY

52   ACKNOWLEDGMENTS

Preface

The one hundred and fiftieth anniversary of the publication of *Leaves of Grass*, the original appearance of which was a transformative moment in the history of American, indeed, world literature, could not be allowed to pass without The New York Public Library and its Henry W. and Albert A. Berg Collection of English and American Literature acknowledging its arrival with an exhibition of at least some of the numerous rare books, photographs, Whitman-annotated proof copies, manuscripts, and correspondence that distinguish the Library's, and the Berg Collection's, Whitman holdings.

An important goal of the exhibition was to display at least one copy of every authorized American edition of *Leaves of Grass* (a score of pirated editions of the 1860–61 edition appeared over the course of twenty years) and of the separate collections of poetry that Whitman later incorporated into *Leaves* and that were published during his lifetime. But space limitations required certain omissions in order that the poem's knotty themes and their complex evolution over the course of decades could be told, and so that at least a generous handful of the Berg's thirty-five Whitman manuscripts (not including over seventy substantive manuscript fragments) could be included, thereby providing a glimpse of Whitman's creative process. These comprise three textually insignificant printings of *Leaves* (the Camden, 1876, edition, essentially a reprint of the 1870–71 edition; the Camden, 1882, reprint of the withdrawn 1881–82 Boston edition; and the Philadelphia, 1889, printing, whose binding Whitman designed), as well as *Passage to India* (though manuscripts of parts of the work are shown) and a few other separate collections. Similarly, though the exhibition contains almost a dozen photographs of Whitman, the dozen others in the Berg could not be accommodated. But the most underrepresented category of the Berg's Whitman material is the more than 350 letters and postcards written in his hand. Whitman was a copious and vivid letter writer, and as one might imagine, these documents provide a richly informative and affecting biographical complement to many of the themes in *Leaves*. But the need to explicate the themes themselves, as well as Whitman's reworking of them through emendation, excision, and the rearrangement of poems, had to take precedence over the desire to document parallel or complementary developments in Whitman's life, so that, in the end, only one Whitman letter was selected for display. This is a letter to his mother, the bulk of which is devoted to describing in detail, in a tone that is characteristically both matter-of-fact and deeply compassionate (and a bit prideful), how he has nursed a young, critically ill soldier out of mortal danger, and which also includes a deeply poignant portrait of Abraham Lincoln, whom he loved and revered, and whom he regularly witnessed riding in the presidential coach through the streets of Washington.

This catalogue's introductory essay, in which evidence of Whitman's homosexuality and racism is presented (based often on the work of others, though the interpretations are largely my own), should shock no one who has, regarding Whitman's homosexuality, honestly read the published poetry, as well as the texts of unexpurgated manuscripts and coded diary entries, and, regarding Whitman's racism, read the offensive passages in at least two of his published prose pieces of the late 1850s and late 1870s, respectively, as well as the relevant correspondence and the manuscripts of several articles, essays, and fragments. Yet such is the power of a benign image when projected upon a great and beloved writer ("the good gray poet," champion of democracy) that something akin to mass hypnosis manifests itself among his readers, and often his literary critics as well, who seem to prefer hero worship to an honest appreciation of the poet and his poetry. To say that Whitman was an advocate of radical democracy is true, simplistically so, but the statement is meaningless without defining what "democracy" meant to him. As it turns out, the answer disqualifies Whitman from admission into the civics-class pantheon of American democratic heroes, whether of the liberal or conservative variety.

First, Whitman's democratic America was to be bound together chiefly by men who were, at least potentially, sexually attracted to each other (to call them "homosexuals" would be anachronistic, and Whitman, often deeply conflicted about his own sexuality and obsessed with the need to see himself as the embodiment of the universal man, would have objected to being labeled by so confining a term). This loving state of affairs, as he saw things, was both right and natural in itself; but it would also help ensure that the haves would not exploit the have-nots, and that the have-nots would not resent the haves. Second, blacks would have no political or civic role of any consequence to play in Whitman's America. He felt that they were by birth intellectually inferior to whites, and because of this belief he was markedly pessimistic about their ability to incorporate themselves fully into American society. This is a large, disfiguring truth about Whitman and it cannot be ignored. He himself warned his readers that he was not merely the affectionate, easy friend they might suppose. In the twelfth poem of the "Calamus" cluster, the series of poems dedicated to "the manly love of comrades," he challenges his readers with a series of rhetorical questions: "Are you the new person drawn toward me, and asking something significant of me? / [. . .] Do you think it so easy to have me become your lover? / [. . .] Do you suppose I am trusty and faithful? / [. . .] Do you see no further than this facade—this smooth and tolerant manner of me?" Third, though he seems to have been benignly tolerant, in person, of those who sub- scribed to the tenets of organized religion, he regarded its various beliefs and practices as, at best, pale, distorted approximations of authentic spirituality (an experience of which, he felt, was the only soil in which radical democracy could take root), and, at worst, as divisive superstitions indulged in by child-adults who needed the authority of tradition or of a religious leader to guide and interpret their lives.

Yes, there is enough in Whitman to offend almost everyone, and he often offends convincingly enough to undermine cherished beliefs—the good gray poet is dangerous. So, when we teach *Leaves of Grass* in grade schools in an attempt to confirm our children in the religion of "democracy," let us remember that like all great poets, Whitman cannot be fully understood by children and adolescents (and by few enough adults), who are congenitally impatient for answers. To paraphrase Rilke, they have not yet learned to live life's questions, often paradoxical and painful. Let us remember, too, that should any child chance to understand Whitman, he or she would immediately become dangerous to his or her parents and teachers ("mind not the cry of the teacher!," he warned in "Song of the Open Road") because s/he will have perceived the falsity of absolutes, without which the parental/pedagogic "yes" and "no" cannot be morally sustained. Whitman himself warns us that he encompasses contradictions; that is, he is a living paradox, subverter of facile assumptions and of the authority of conventional pieties, such as the superiority of "my religion," or "my country," to yours, though Whitman himself believed that America had a special role to play in the world as an exemplar of radical democracy.

Yet such is the purity of Whitman's affection for the unseen reader, and such is the simplicity and directness of his speech (for, more than any English-language poet before him, and perhaps since, his poetry is heard in the mind as the intimately conversational spoken word), that arguments and dialectic are rendered irrelevant. The authenticity of Whitman's experience of the cosmos and all that it contains—rivers, clouds, stars, animals, cruelty, compassion, and, especially, his own and other soul/bodies journeying down the open road—as a unitary, organic entity, and his desire to impart this experience to the reader, is palpable. The only way to convey a sense of this immediacy in an exhibition is to select openings that embody the best of *Leaves of Grass* (not all of it is gold), which means that, though many of the poems in *Leaves* are represented here, none are so much as "Song of Myself," "I Sing the Body Electric," "Song of the Open Road," and "Crossing Brooklyn Ferry." The last poem is the source of the exhibition's, and this book's, title, and appears in the following passage: "I am with you, you men and women of a generation, or ever so many generations hence, / I project myself, also I return—I am with you, and know how it is." This ability to convince us that, indeed, "I am with you," and that his companionship "shall be good health" to us, is the living proof of Whitman's gift, which is to see the world this moment, as it is, and to see that it is good.

Leaves of Grass.

I CELEBRATE myself,
And what I assume you shall assume,
For every atom belonging to me as good belongs to you.

I loafe and invite my soul,
I lean and loafe at my ease .... observing a spear of summer grass.

Houses and rooms are full of perfumes .... the shelves are crowded with perfumes,
I breathe the fragrance myself, and know it and like it,
The distillation would intoxicate me also, but I shall not let it.

The atmosphere is not a perfume .... it has no taste of the distillation .... it is
    odorless,
It is for my mouth forever .... I am in love with it,
I will go to the bank by the wood and become undisguised and naked,
I am mad for it to be in contact with me.

The smoke of my own breath,
Echos, ripples, and buzzed whispers .... loveroot, silkthread, crotch and vine,
My respiration and inspiration .... the beating of my heart .... the passing of blood
    and air through my lungs,
The sniff of green leaves and dry leaves, and of the shore and darkcolored sea-
    rocks, and of hay in the barn,
The sound of the belched words of my voice .... words loosed to the eddies of
    the wind,
A few light kisses .... a few embraces .... a reaching around of arms,
The play of shine and shade on the trees as the supple boughs wag,
The delight alone or in the rush of the streets, or along the fields and hillsides,
The feeling of health .... the full-noon trill .... the song of me rising from bed
    and meeting the sun.

The twelve poems comprising the 1855 *Leaves of Grass*
(the first page of which is seen here) were untitled.
The first three lines of the first poem establish one of
Whitman's cardinal affirmations: that in celebrating
himself, he is celebrating all of humanity, since
everything in the cosmos partakes of everything else.

"I Am with [Some of] You"

I am with you, you men and women of a generation, or ever so many
    generations hence,
I project myself—also I return—I am with you, and know how it is.
Just as you feel when you look on the river and sky, so I felt,
Just as any of you is one of a living crowd, I was one of a crowd [. . .]
— "Sun-Down Poem," 1856 [later, "Crossing Brooklyn Ferry"]

Of all the epochal achievements in American literary history, Walt
Whitman's publication of *Leaves of Grass*, on July 4, 1855, must be
regarded as one of the more improbable. The thirty-six-year-old former
Long Island schoolteacher, who himself received only six years of
formal education, had been many things, none of which, certainly in
the mid-nineteenth century, promised literary distinction: a printer's
apprentice and typesetter; a purple-prose Brooklyn journalist; a
harshly polemical newspaper editor; and the author of a hackneyed,
sentimental temperance novel. Moreover, he had shown no indication
that he was capable of revolutionizing English poetics, creating a
style of conversational and declamatory free verse embodied in long,
irregularly metered lines, or that he could use that syle to express
with such seeming ease the radically unorthodox combination of
spiritual, sexual, and political sensibilities—for Whitman, the three
were inextricably intertwined—that makes the first edition of *Leaves
of Grass*, and many of the new poems that appeared in the subsequent
editions, as much a spiritual teaching as a pioneering literary work.

  Whitman would labor over *Leaves of Grass* steadily for the
rest of his life, publishing at least eight versions, depending on one's

definition of "version," in nine editions, or several more if one includes parts of the work that were first published separately. The successive editions reflect a virtually unrelenting process of emendation, occasional excision, and, most importantly, rearrangement (which ceased with the 1881–82 edition) and addition (including the addition of titles, which the poems received only in the second, 1856, edition), so that by the time of Whitman's death, in 1892, *Leaves of Grass* had grown fourfold in size, and the work's most famous and most powerful poem, later titled, successively, "A Poem of Walt Whitman, an American," "Walt Whitman," and, most famously, "Song of Myself," had been trans-formed, with many dismembered stanzas planted amid more recently composed verses and poems. The 1855 poems that appeared in the 1856 edition were now titled, and were joined by twenty new ones; in all, the 1856 edition contained more than twice as many lines as that of 1855. The third edition, published in 1860–61, became the best known in Whitman's day and, with 120 new poems, contained twice the number of lines as the 1856 edition. But in subsequent editions—1867, 1871–72 (i.e., 1870), 1876 (a virtual reprint of the 1871–72 edition), 1881–82, 1889, and 1891–92—the amount of new material would dimin-ish almost exponentially with each successive edition, and, with many notable exceptions, so would Whitman's inspiration.

In the 1860–61 edition, Whitman introduced thematic groups of poems ("clusters," he called them), the two most important being "Enfans d'Adam" (later titled "Children of Adam") and "Calamus," which were about, respectively, heterosexual love and "the manly love of comrades." This innovation also marked the beginning of a lifelong process of rearranging poems that had first appeared in previous editions, sometimes scattering new ones among them, as he attempted to give the ever-changing face of *Leaves* the appearance of a book whose many poems and clusters were thematically united. In this cause, he also changed or excised words, phrases, and lines, in an effort to marry stylistic uniformity to thematic unity, often to the poems' detriment. (One of the many instances of Whitman's emendatory impulse undermining his poetry is the 1891–92 text of "Crossing Brooklyn Ferry," which became a more controlled, less passionate, and less intimate poem than the original, 1856 "Sun-Down Poem,"

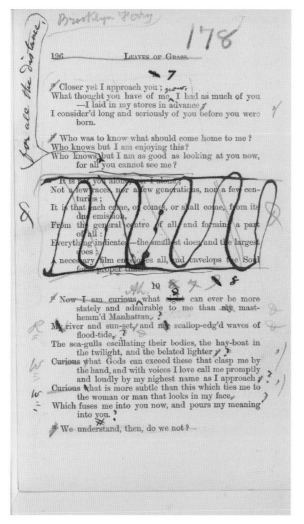

or, for that matter, the 1881–82 "Crossing.") As for the separately published books of poetry that Whitman inserted into *Leaves*, most of these had been composed in response to special circumstances, or with a particular theme in mind. For instance, with few exceptions, the poems in the 1865 *Drum-Taps* and *Sequel to Drum-Taps* (the latter titled "In Memoriam" when it was incorporated into the 1867 *Leaves*) were about, or related to, the Civil War. *Passage to India*, a much shorter collection than Whitman had intended, was begun as a companion piece to *Leaves*, to explore the subject of the soul's journey toward the Brahmanic Divine (though, in truth, this had been a theme in much of the 1855 *Leaves*), but he proved unable to write enough poems in this vein, and so *Passage*, too, was incorporated into the larger work. Some of Whitman's occasional poems retained their independence and, with few exceptions, have drifted to the outermost orbits of our literary awareness; *Leaves of Grass* was the great sun into which most of his verse was drawn.

Today, 150 years after its first appearance, *Leaves of Grass* remains disturbingly honest, demanding, unique, and inimitable. Its poetic modes are various:

extended passages of lyrical beauty, usually describing a nature scene or invoking a series of nature metaphors, a gift that did not weaken until the later years: "Lilac and star and bird twined with the chant of my soul, / There in the fragrant pines and the cedars dusk and dim" ("When Lilacs Last in the Dooryard Bloom'd");

self-revelations simply worded, naked and unsentimental, free of self-censure or self-praise: "Hurrying with the modern crowd, as eager and fickle as any, / Hot toward one I hate, ready in my madness to knife him" ("Song of Myself"[1]), sometimes seeming to convey a truth beyond the expressive power of artistic intention: "Solitary at midnight in my back yard, my thoughts gone from me a long while, / Walking the old hills of Judea with the beautiful gentle god by my side" ("Song of Myself");

lacerating or joyful declamations about, respectively, the social and natural orders; most seductively, the assured, intimately conversational voice, urgent with immediacy, imparting a sense that the poet is looking out at us, into us, from his leaves of grass: "I am with you, you men and women of a generation, or ever so many generations hence, / [. . .] I am with you, and know how it is" ("Sun-Down Poem"), and we into ourselves: "It is you talking just as much as myself" ("Sun-Down Poem")—an achievement still unmatched in English poetry;

and, primarily in the editions following that of 1860–61, ever-widening wastelands of abstract speechifying and list-making—Whitman at his most intentionally metaphysical and prosaically all-inclusive.

Even so, some of the notorious lists, especially in the first-edition text, are vividly phrased, their subjects juxtaposed to develop a theme, or to surprise, building in tension until they culminate in dramatic and moving denouements. And, despite its flaws, *Leaves of Grass*, certainly in its first incarnation, is one of a very few long poems in American literature that can be called "inspired."

Like many inspired works, the first edition text is a knot of paradoxes, often presented in Zarathustra-like epigrams,[2] such as, "I bring what you much need, yet always have" (from the poem later titled "A Song for Occupations"); or, "What is called good is perfect, and what is called sin is just as perfect" (from the poem later titled "To Think of Time"). Whitman can move rapidly from self-celebration to self-extinction; from a reveling in the senses to an embrace of death: "Has anyone supposed it lucky to be born? / I hasten to inform him or her it is just as lucky to die, and I know it" ("Song of Myself"); from ardent description of male muscularity at rest and in supple flexion— "the flex of his waist and knees [. . .] / The strong sweet supple quality he has strikes through the cotton and flannel" ("I Sing the Body Electric")—to the female body's "divine nimbus" of "fierce undeniable attraction": "Hair, bosom, hips, bend of legs, negligent falling hands [. . .] / [. . .] loveflesh swelling and deliciously aching" ("I Sing the Body Electric"); from the exaltation of a specific natural wonder, whether a mountain, "the mossy scabs of the wormfence," or a handful of grass brought to him by a questioning child: "the grass is itself a child [. . .] / [. . .] the beautiful uncut hair of graves" ("Song of Myself"); to a distinction-erasing, momentary emergence into cosmic oneness.[3]

The importance of Whitman's "oneness experience" (or "attitude," into which his poetry falls when he attempts to stimulate inspiration through memory) in the composition of *Leaves of Grass* cannot be overemphasized, though historical forces and the culture of his time played a large, indeed, ever-larger role as the poem evolved; and, of course, as is true of any poet, his work was also shaped by the distinctive forces and dualities of his nature and background: Deist/Quaker; town/country; artisan/literary dandy; bohemian barfly/exalter of family life; hectoring orator/whispering prophet; strident journalist/lyric guru. But his conviction that the entire cosmos, including human consciousness, is an indivisible, organic whole animates virtually all of his poetry and much of his later prose, and is the explicit subject of most of the 1855 *Leaves*.

Despite this cosmic vision, often expressed through the microcosm of an acute attention to apparently mundane scenes and events, *Leaves of Grass* is also an epic—that is, a tale about a particular hero who seeks his particular destiny. In Whitman's epic, the hero is, at once, both Whitman himself and the ideal America of his prophetic imagination, together tramping the "open road." Unlike the heros of classical epics, Whitman's and America's destiny is not to return home, like Ulysses to Ithaca, but to "tramp a perpetual journey," mostly in joy, at least in the first edition, but occasionally in sadness and frustration, emotions which found expression with increasing frequency in subsequent editions. Despite the thematic similarities of *Leaves of Grass* with the epic form, Whitman, in his preface to the first edition, explicitly refused to apply the designation "epic" to the poetry of the "new" American poet, i.e., himself. But this was because he found the conventional epic narrative too straightforward and explicit in its intentions for a poet whose verse was, as he put it in the 1855 preface, "indirect." What he had experienced and wanted to recount defied linear narrative and explication. Of course, he recognized the existence of linear progress in the technological realm, and he would write with great enthusiasm about such globe-shrinking engineering feats as the joining of the continental United States by the Union Pacific and Western Pacific railroads, the laying of the transatlantic cable, and the opening of the Suez Canal, all of which he celebrates

In the 1850s, Ralph Waldo Emerson (1803–1882), pictured below, was, after Longfellow, America's most eminent writer. He was also, with Henry David Thoreau and several other New England writers and philosophers, a formulator of Transcendentalism, which taught that the cosmos was a unified, living entity. Emerson called for the creation of a new, robust American literature, owing nothing to European forms and sensibilities, and characterized by energy, directness, and an exploration of eternal truths, rather than by a polished style. Whitman saw himself as an avatar of Emerson's prescriptions, and here, in "Emerson, An Appreciation," ca. 1854, he praises Emerson's writings: "The superiority of Emerson's writings is in their character—they mean something. He may be obscure, but he is certain. [. . .] He represents the freeman, America, the individual." The following year, Whitman sent Emerson and a few other well-known American writers a copy of *Leaves of Grass*, with a request that they offer their opinions of it. Only Emerson replied, famously predicting a glorious future for its author.

17

18

In this portion of the title poem of Whitman's 1871 collection, *Passage to India*, the poet imagines himself aboard a Union Pacific train: "In one again (different, yet thine all thine O soul the same), / I see over my continent the Pacific railroad / I see continual trains of cars winding along the Platte / . . ."

in "Passage to India," the title poem of the 1871 collection that was immediately incorporated into the 1871–72 edition of *Leaves of Grass*.

But the spiritual journey of which Whitman writes, and upon which, he says, each individual is embarked, is not linear ("I do not talk of the beginning or end"); that is, salvation does not lie at the end of the road. Rather, it inheres in the journeying itself (Whitman recalled that as a young man he "cross'd and recross'd [the East River, by ferry] merely for pleasure"), whose essence is a process of moment-to-moment awakening: "There was never any more inception than there is now, / [. . .] / [. . .] And will never be any more perfection than there is now" ("Song of Myself"); and "Happiness not in another place but this place . . not for another hour, but this hour" ("A Song for Occupations").[4] Moreover, this happiness dwells in each soul/body ("the soul is not more than the body, / [. . .] the body is not more than the soul"), and since the individual soul/body is part of the cosmic soul/material universe, "not [even] God, is greater to one than one's-self is" ("Song of Myself"), a declaration he had made somewhat professorially, in the 1855 preface: "It is also not consistent with the reality of the soul to admit that there is anything in the known universe more divine than men and women."

Such affirmations, in which *Leaves of Grass* abounds (for instance, "Divine am I inside and out, and I make holy whatever I touch or am touched from," from "Song of Myself"), are Whitman's attempts to bring us, indirectly, as he promised in his preface, to an experience of the higher Self by shocking and frustrating the thought process, which sees the world in dualistic categories, such as body/mind or soul, inner/outer, God/not-God. Usually, Whitman uses the word "God" as a signifier for a truth that lies beyond verbal expression, as in "God comes a loving bedfellow and sleeps at my side all night" ("Song of Myself"), which in this instance means that truth was expressed as sexual love. But, at least in the first edition text, he has no use for the conventional concept of a Supreme Being—a personal, yet infinite, consciousness—since in the infinite, eternal unity of which he speaks there exists no divine identity separate from the world or from the individual soul/bodies that inhabit it. Whitman warns his readers away from indulging their intellectual curiosity about ultimate, unanswerable questions: "And I call to mankind, Be not curious about God, / For I who am curious about each am not curious about God, / [. . .] I hear and behold God in every object, yet I understand God not in the least, / Nor do I understand who there can be more wonderful than myself."

The "myself" of which Whitman speaks in such contexts is not the ego, but what the Hindu Vedas, Upanishads, and other Eastern spiritual traditions call "the higher Self," an energy manifest not only in each sentient being, but in trees, rocks, air—indeed, in every atom of the cosmos. (This is not to deny that *Leaves of Grass* contains numerous examples of genuine, exuberant egotism, as Whitman cheerfully admitted: "I know perfectly well my own egotism.") Near the beginning of "Song of Myself," Whitman distinguishes between the accidents of his personality, formed by his conditioning and its reaction to experience, and what he called "the Me myself":

People I meet . . . . . the effect upon me of my early life . . . . of the ward
    and city I live in . . . . of the nation,
The latest news [. . .]
My dinner, dress, associates, looks, business, compliments, dues,
The real or fancied indifference of some man or woman I love,
The sickness of one of my folks—or of myself [. . .]
They come to me days and nights and go from me again,
But they are not Me myself.

Apart from the pulling and hauling stands what I am,
Stands amused, complacent, compassionate, unitary [. . .]

This "Me" is what Whitman referred to when he wrote, "Divine am I inside and out."[5] For Whitman, God is within (i.e., human consciousness awakened) as well as without (i.e., the physical world, including the human body); but since he sees no distinction between inner and outer, all that exists is God, which makes "God" an unnecessary concept, at least in the first edition of *Leaves*. Whitman saw as his chief duty to talk, not about God, but about his own Oneness experience and the spiritual journey that it had initiated.

Allusions to this never-ending spiritual journey are scattered throughout the 1855 *Leaves*, as well as in some of the new poem clusters introduced into the later editions (it is the title theme of the 1856 "Poem of the Road"), but are formulated most tellingly in "Song of Myself." Here we learn that the appropriate state in which to undertake the perpetual journey is an almost passive form of attention: "All truths wait in all things, / They neither hasten their own delivery nor resist it, / They do not need the obstetric forceps of the surgeon." This attentiveness also includes a kind of listening in which the categories of "inner" and "outer" disappear, and sounds become part of the listener himself: "I think I will do nothing for a long time but listen, / And accrue what I hear into myself . . . . and let sounds contribute toward me." Because Whitman understands that we may not be aware that we have been journeying on a spiritual "open road" ("Perhaps you have been on it since you were born, and did not know, / Perhaps it is everywhere on water and on land"), he will do all he can to awaken us to this fact—that is, he will "wash the gum" from our sleep-filled eyes and point out to us the heretofore unseen "landscapes of continents" and the "plain public road" that passes through them. But, though he can show us the road, he cannot travel it for us ("Not I, nor any one else can travel that road for you, / You must travel it for yourself"). Extending the water image, he exhorts the reader to be a "bold swim-mer" who joyfully plunges into the sea. He himself is a "teacher of [spiritual, as well as physical] athletes" who revels in being bested by his disciples. Bringing the passage to a dramatic culmination, he declares, "He most honors my style who learns under it to destroy the teacher," which is uncannily reminiscent of the Zen saying, "If you meet the Buddha on the road, kill him."

Whitman's great hope, indeed, his expectation (at least in 1855), was that his readers, the new breed of American men and women of whom he sang, would join him in a spirit of independent explo-ration on a perpetual journey down the open road of existence, thereby transforming America and, eventually, the world: each one alone, though not lonely, in self-realization—a true individual (i.e., not dependent on social conventions and received opinion)—yet tramping the road united in purpose with other Americans; each individual observing carefully, and learning from his or her own experience that all consciousness is one, an awareness that creates a deep sympathy with the individual entities that comprise the cosmos. As Whitman wrote in one of the eleven manuscript prefaces to *Leaves* that remained unpublished during his lifetime, "Small is my theme, yet the greatest—namely One's-self, a simple, separate person. That, for the use of the New World, I sing."

Should his readers undertake the journey in this independent spirit, says Whitman, they may discover that truth is alive in all things, great and small—"a leaf of grass is no less than the journeywork of the stars" ("Song of Myself")—a discovery which will arouse sympathy in each of them for all whom they see. Sympathy is a crucial word in Whitman's poetic lexicon. In the earliest extant draft for "Song of Myself" he wrote, "Greater than wires of iron or treaties, or even strong material interest is Sympathy." Sympathy is not pity, nor sentimental identification, but an insight that reveals another's consciousness to be essentially the same as one's own, which means that all human beings, regardless of their natural gifts or station in life, are equal. It also means that each human being has the capacity to achieve this insight. (Those who do not are consigned to the status of a walking corpse: "whoever walks a furlong without sympathy walks to his own funeral.") Rebelling against the dominant cultural and religious traditions that exalted the artist or spiritual master as a superior being, Whitman declares that the true poet, artist, and seer are not, and do not feel themselves, better than others, as he stressed in the 1855 preface: "The message of great poets to each man and woman are [*sic*], Come to us on equal terms, Only then can you understand us"; and in "Song of Myself" he assures his readers, "It is you talking just as much as myself . . . . I act as the tongue of you, / It was tied in your mouth . . . . in mine it begins to be loosened."

This vision of essential equality became Whitman's first political principle, though he was still too much a creature of his time and his personal prejudices to follow all of its implications to their conclusions. However, his references in *Leaves of Grass* to the equality of women and men admit no equivocation. Even in his preface he takes the extraordinary step of referring to both women and men as workers ("the noble character of the young mechanics and of all free American workmen and workwomen") and asserts that the unity of American workers in affection and common purpose ("the general ardor and friendliness and enterprise") is based on "the perfect equality of the female with the male." Later in the preface, he again mentions women alongside men in their capacity as laborers and artisans: "If you are a workman or workwoman I stand as nigh as the nighest that works in the same shop." Such workplace references to women, unremarkable to a modern reader, would, in mid-nineteenth-century America, which preferred to idealize women even as it restricted them legally and socially, have marked its writer as a women's rights advocate. Almost equally impressive, on each occasion in the preface that Whitman praises or mentions men, he praises or mentions women; for instance, "he [the poet] offers the sweet firmfibred meat that grows men and women"; and "he sees eternity in men and women . . . he does not see men and women as dreams or dots."[6]

Leaves of Grass itself is also filled with similar constructions, such as: "all the men ever born are also my brothers . . . . and the women my sisters and lovers"; "make short account of neuters and geldings, and favor men and women fully equipped" ("Song of Myself"); and "The wife—and she is not one jot less than the husband, / The daughter—and she is just as good as the son, / The mother— and she is every bit as much as the father" ("A Song for Occupations").[7] This last passage is especially significant, since in mid-nineteenth-century America the home was, even more than today, a very private space in which the male dominated (as husband and father), or (as son) was valued more highly than the household's women, and in which a woman first internalized her inferior status.

The preface also portrays women as *political* beings. Referring to the American people's ability to discern whether or not any contribution or proposed innovation in the fields of literature, commerce, national defense, or law is worthy of their country, Whitman mentions women alongside men as engaged citizens, deciding that "Whether or no the sign appears from the mouths of the people, it throbs a live interrogation in every freeman's and freewoman's heart after that which passes by or this built to remain. Is it uniform with my country?" "Poem of Procreation" (later titled "A Woman Waits for Me"), which first appeared in the 1856 edition of *Leaves* and is best known for its depiction of Whitman as sexual athlete ("I pour the stuff to start sons and daughters fit for These States—I press with slow rude muscle, / I brace myself effectually—I listen to no entreaties, / I dare not withdraw till I deposit what has so long accumulated in me"),[8] also contains his assertion that he (the ideal American man) regards America's women as "not one jot less than I am." The women of Whitman's America are not the delicate, idealized figures of mid-nineteenth-century poetry, but amorous and intelligent Amazons who "know how to swim, row, ride, wrestle, shoot, run, strike, retreat, advance, resist, defend themselves, / They are ultimate in their own right—they are calm, clear, well-possessed of themselves." Whitman's assertion that women need to be able to defend themselves told women's rights advocates that he understood how dependence on a man for physical safety might render a woman psychologically dependent, and also that a woman might need to defend herself within the home, against the very man who was her supposed defender.

Referring to women in their capacity as laborers and artisans, mentioning them whenever men, in the aggregate, are mentioned, asserting their equality with men in the home, and advocating that they cultivate the skills of self-defense, all of this identified Whitman as a champion of women's rights, a status that was further attested to by support for him from such activists as Abby Price, Paulina Wright Davis, and Sarah Tyndale. As some of his critics have noted, what Whitman does *not* do in *Leaves of Grass* is imagine an America in which, for instance, women can vote and stand for elective office, attend universities, manage railroads, and join the professions, and in which married women can own property, though as early as 1847 he editorialized against this legal restriction. But in large part, Whitman's political reticence regarding women was a function of his poetic intentions—he was not trying to write a political tract, though he was often consciously writing in a political context. Whitman speaks prophetically of an America in which spiritual and sexual freedom will overthrow the old order and establish a radical democratic society in which social, regional, economic, and political conflicts will be harmonized, but he had no interest in setting forth in practical detail the manner in which these harmonizations would be achieved.

Equally radical and threatening to the social and political order was the portrayal of women in *Leaves of Grass* as erotic beings, not merely as childbearers. Though common enough in the period's popular pornography, this had never before been attempted in serious American literature. Whitman's women not only arouse sexual desire in men, but experience it themselves, as in this passage from "Song of Myself," describing a wealthy and lonely young woman spying on naked male swimmers as she fantasizes about them:

An unseen hand also passed over their bodies,
It descended tremblingly from their temples and ribs.
The young men float on their backs, their white bellies swell to the sun . . . .
    they do
not ask who seizes fast to them,
They do not know who puffs and declines with pendant and bending arch,
They do not think whom they souse with spray.

Though Whitman has been criticized, most wittily by D. H. Lawrence, for portraying American women exclusively as procreative machines (*Leaves of Grass* does contain numerous descriptions of ideal Whitmanian women breeding with ideal Whitmanian men for the good of the democratic state, a vision that disturbed the women's rights theoretician and activist Elizabeth Cady Stanton, as it does many modern readers), this charge, as we have seen, is unfair. True, Whitman does not write of a time when American women will be captains of commerce and Supreme Court justices. But he consistently asserts their equality with men and portrays them as strong, independent individuals, capable of mastering their own fates and of contributing not just healthy babies, but their talents and energy, to the national effort that will realize his vision of a renewed and unified America.

Yet as strong as was Whitman's conviction that gender equality and the free expression of sexual desire between men and women were both just and natural, and, hence, to be advocated,[9] it was exceeded by his commitment to the free expression of men's love and sexual attraction for each other. An accurate appreciation of Whitman's vision of radical democracy and national unity must recognize that, in his mind, the realization of these ideals would be based primarily on what he called "the manly love of comrades." Exactly what Whitman meant by "manly love" in his own life has, until relatively recently, been the subject of considerable disagreement and confusion, abetted by Whitman himself, who was afraid to admit his homosexual feelings (homosexuality, as a scientific or social category, did not even exist until the end of the nineteenth century), and who emphatically asserted to the English homosexual rights advocate Edward Carpenter, who pressed him on this point, that he had never engaged in sexual acts with men. Today, few critics would deny the homosexual content of most of the "manly love" poems, as well as of many passages in "Song of Myself" and in other poems of *Leaves*. Still, Whitman sometimes managed to cover his sexuality, just barely, in the cloak of ardent friendship, abetted by a culture in which male (or, for that matter, female) friendships were often accompanied by physical gestures of affection that today would generally be interpreted as sexual, but which, in mid-nineteenth-century America, did not necessarily imply more than deep emotional attachment.

The 1860–61 edition of *Leaves of Grass* contains, as mentioned earlier, a cluster of poems that celebrate heterosexual love ("Enfans d'Adam") and another that celebrate homosexual love between men ("Calamus").[10] Characteristic of the homosexuality in the "Calamus" poems are such lines as, "When he whom I love travels with me or sits a long while holding me by the hand, / [. . .] I am satisfied, / He ahold of my hand has completely satisfied me" ("Of the Terrible Doubt of Appearances"). In other instances, the sexual content is even plainer, though, admittedly, still only implied: "For the one I love most lay sleeping by me under the same cover in the cool night, / [. . .] his face was inclined toward me, / And his arm lay lightly around my breast— And that night I was happy" ("When I Heard at the Close of the Day"). Plainer still is the manuscript text of "Once I Pass'd Through a Populous City," a poem that describes Whitman's New Orleans love affair with a man, though he changed the lover's gender to female in the published version, placing it among the "Enfans d'Adam" cluster:

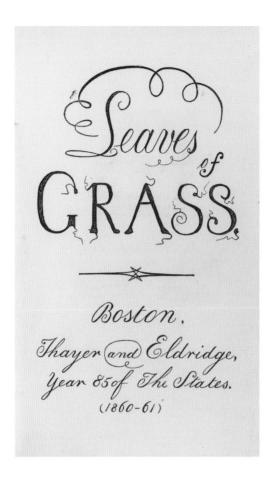

In February 1860, the Boston abolitionist publishers William Thayer and Charles Eldridge asked Whitman if they might issue a new edition of *Leaves of Grass*. Whitman, who had been writing new poems profusely, eagerly went to Boston to negotiate a contract and present his design for the book. He used cursive script on the title page, probably in an attempt to establish a more intimate relationship with the reader. Years later, in "So Long!," he would write, "This is no book; / Who touches this, touches a man."

"Yet now of all that city I remember only a woman I casually met there who detain'd me for love of me, / Day by day and night by night we were together, / [. . .] / I remember I say only that woman who passionately clung to me [. . .]."[11] But homosexual attraction held a significance for Whitman beyond erotic pleasure or deep friendship. He saw "the manly love of comrades" as a necessary condition for the realization of his vision of a democratic America, believing that "camerados" (the word may be a punning combination of "comrade" and "camera," a vessel that holds what it sees, just as a lover holds the image of his beloved) would not exploit each other for financial and political gain if they were bound to each other by love and "adhesiveness," a phrenological term that he employed to signify male

28

The frontispiece engraving (based on an 1854 photograph) for the first edition of *Leaves of Grass*, showing Whitman in the garb of an artisan (above), was intended to enhance the poem's representation of the poet as an Everyman. But for the 1860–61 edition Whitman chose an engraving, based on a portrait by his friend Charles Hine, showing himself in Byronic attire (below), conforming to conventional contemporary notions about a poet's appearance. Whitman's choice of the Hine portrait (which he never used again) may reflect a desire for general acceptance as a "genuine" poet, which had been denied him by most critics.

homosexual attraction. In the preface to the 1876 edition of *Leaves of Grass*, he wrote that "The special meaning of the *Calamus* cluster mainly resides in its Political significance," a connection that he made explicit in "For You O Democracy": "Come, I will make the continent indissoluble, / . . . With the love of comrades, / With the life-long love of comrades."

Does this mean that Whitman believed that *only* men who saw each other as potential sexual partners were capable of knitting together the United States? Perhaps. But because of his often con- flicted attitude toward his own sexuality, the question may never have presented itself to him so explicitly, or he may not have allowed it to do so. Yes, he regarded his sexual urges as cause for celebration, but also, occasionally, for regret, the latter emotion being intensified by his need to see and present himself as the ideal American male— champion procreator. A diary entry of 1870 contains a self admonishment not to, once again, become too attached to a young man to whom he is drawn by this "diseased, feverish disproportionate adhesiveness." Whether or not the term "diseased" reflects self-loathing born of shame, or is merely a more intense correlative to "feverish" and "disproportionate," this passage should be understood not only as the characteristic complaint of any besotted, would-be lover, but as an expression of frustration at being unable to express his sexuality fully and openly. One may surmise that his partially regretted and incompletely fulfilled homosexual desires intensified the ardor of his male friendships, an experience that he might, with good reason, assume was shared by many other men. So why should he not believe that many others also possessed his own capacity at least for friendship, if nothing more? This granted, why should he not also believe that a substantial number of men, encouraged properly by the right poet/ prophet, might form themselves into a continent-spanning community of comrades that would replace competition and exploitation with affection (and perhaps more; the matter need not have been settled in his mind) and thereby "make the continent indissoluble"?

But regardless of how one chooses to define "manly love" in a Whitmanian political context the country's most threatening division in the 1850s, in Whitman's view and in reality, was not between men

growing,
All alone stood it, and the moss
hung down from the branches,
Without any companion it grew
there, glistening out with joyous
leaves of dark green,
And its look, rude, unbending, lusty,
made me think of myself;
But I wondered how it could
utter joyous leaves, standing alone
there without its friend, its
lover — For I knew I could
not;
And I plucked a twig with a certain
number of leaves upon it and
twined around it a little moss,
and brought it away — And I
have placed it in sight in m
room,

The famous thirteen-line poem "I Saw in Louisiana a Live-Oak Growing," expressing Whitman's loneliness after being forsaken by his lover, was published as number 20 in the "Calamus" cluster, in the 1860–61 edition. It was titled "Live Oak, with Moss," in the manuscript notebook of the same name, which contains the twelve original "Calamus" poems in an order that clearly recounts the history of a homosexual love affair.

who were "comradely" and those who weren't, but between slave states and free states. Whitman was too canny an observer of the political landscape (as is attested to by his newspaper articles and essays) to believe that this division was amenable to healing simply through the comradeship of Northern and Southern white men. In fact, it is difficult to find in Whitman's poetry or prose any attempt to formulate a political solution to the division of America over the slavery issue. His failure to do so may be attributed primarily to his viewing the cruel injustice of slavery as a lesser evil than the consequence of forcibly abolishing it. This is not to deny Whitman's sympathy for the slave's plight, which he movingly portrayed several times in the 1855 *Leaves*, emphasizing the slave's humanity and dignity. Also, he voiced opposition to slavery in a large number of editorials and essays, from the late 1840s through the 1870s.

The depth of Whitman's repugnance for slavery and his sympathy with the slave's suffering is expressed most famously in three stanzas of the 1855 edition's second section, later titled "The Sleepers." Here, Whitman assumes the persona of a young, angry, black slave named Lucifer, who vows vengeance on his master for having oppressed and defiled him and his family, and for having sadistically separated him from his woman. Employing one of the most powerful and vivid metaphors in *Leaves*, Lucifer ends his monologue with a warning to the slaveholding South that he is a black whale (in 1851, Herman Melville had published *Moby-Dick*, the tale of a white whale that wreaks vengeance on his mad hunters) and, though not yet fully awakened into awareness, is deadly dangerous when provoked: "Now the vast bulk that is the whale's bulk . . . . it seems mine, / Warily, sportsman! Though I lie so sleepy and sluggish, my tap is death." Today, a fictional leap into the mind of the Other may not seem daring or even unusual, but the uniqueness and courageousness of Whitman's "Lucifer" must be given their due.[12] For the first time, a white writer had adopted the persona of an angry black slave; moreover, he had done so sympathetically, helping the reader to understand and not condemn the slave's murderous rage against his cruel master and against the injustices and humiliations of slavery itself. This radical act Whitman had dared at a time when slave revolts were rife across the

South, which made the imagery and sentiments of the "Lucifer" poem seem recklessly provoc-ative even to many Northerners.

Perhaps equally offensive to many white readers, Whitman had challenged the legitimacy of the American Church in naming the slave "Lucifer," after the angel who rebelled against God ("Lucifer" was also a play on a popular nickname for the radical, anti-slavery Democrats).[13] For at least a century, ministers, priests, and their "scholarly" apologists, primarily in the South, but occasionally in the North as well, commonly explicated certain passages in Genesis in a manner that attempted to prove that the enslavement of black Africans was divinely sanctioned. Since white America had trans-formed God into the ultimate slave master, Whitman was saying, the slave's only choice was to assume the role of rebellious Lucifer.

Paradoxically, despite the obvious sympathy Whitman expressed in "Song of Myself" for the slave's suffering and rage ("I am the hounded slave . . . . I wince at the bite of the dogs, / Hell and despair are upon me, / [. . .] I fall on the weeds and stones, / The riders spur their unwilling horses and haul close, / [. . .] they beat me violently over the head with their whip-stocks"), he also proclaimed his sympathy (*not* approval) for the slave master, though not as vividly or as extensively. (Among a long list of identities that Whitman claims for himself in "Song of Myself" are those of "A southerner soon as a northerner, planter nonchalant and hospitable.") Because Whitman sees both slave and master as essentially one in consciousness (though they are unaware of it), he can anticipate the day when "The call of the slave is one with the master's call . . and the master salutes the slave" ("The Sleepers"). But this harmonious vision is not to be realized through political struggle (at least, there is no mention of it in *Leaves of Grass*). Rather, it will come about as a consequence of the slave's and the master's spiritual awakening. Whitman's vision of all-in-oneness will not allow him to perpetuate divisions among human beings, even by condemning the wicked: "It [i.e., the spiritual meal he has prepared] is for the wicked just the same as the righteous" ("Song of Myself"). Instead, he maintains sympathy with both perpetrator and victim, trusting that eventually the two will be reconciled in an awareness of each other's humanity/divinity. This is one reason why

32

neither in the first nor in subsequent editions of *Leaves* does Whitman advocate abolition as a *political* imperative.

But in explaining Whitman's *poetic* reticence on abolition (he explicitly opposed abolition in editorials while editor of the *Brooklyn Eagle*, from 1846 until his dismissal, in January 1848) one must recognize that, aside from his refusal to introduce politics into his song of the unitary cosmos, two other powerful motives were at work. The first (as indicated above) was his fear of dividing the Union and precipitating a civil war. Most of Whitman's explicitly anti-slavery writings, outside of *Leaves of Grass*, focus on the *spread* of slavery. From the prose writings published both before and after the first appearance of *Leaves*, and during the Civil War, we know that as strongly as he opposed abolition, he also opposed the spread of slavery to the free states and territories. (He was fired from the *Brooklyn Eagle* because its publisher, a pro-slavery Democrat, was incensed by his free-soil editorials.) So deep was this conviction that, in late 1848, he founded a newspaper, the *Brooklyn Freeman*, dedicated to the free-soil cause. But his opposition to the spread of slavery owed as much to his fear that slave labor would depreciate wages for whites, as it did to his repugnance for the suffering that slavery inflicted. Without question, he regarded the return of runaway slaves in free states to their Southern owners as a terrible cruelty; one of the more moving portions of "Song of Myself" is a fictional account of his sheltering a runaway slave (as in the previously quoted passage beginning "I am the hounded slave"). But he could not support the political movement to abolish slavery, since slavery seemed to him a less grievous evil than the inevitable civil war that would follow a government-backed attempt to legislate and enforce abolition.

Only a unified America would enable the citizenry to fulfill its sacred destiny—to demonstrate to the world that self-realized men and women, of diverse geographic, ethnic, and economic backgrounds, could together build a new culture based on enlightened affection and freely expressed sexual attraction, of men and women for each other, and of men for men. This vision of unity remained a cherished goal his entire life. In 1891, the year of his death, looking back on the creation and growth of *Leaves*, he wrote in *Lippincott's Magazine*, "One of my dearest objects in my poetic expression has been to combine these Forty-Four United States into One Identity, fused, equal, and independent." But this golden vision could be realized only if the country remained united. After the war's outbreak and in its aftermath, his memory of the horrors that he had witnessed as a nurse, tending both Union and Confederate troops, intensified his desire for reconciliation between North and South. The occupation of the South by Union troops was anathema to him, and though he grudgingly conceded its short-term necessity, he wanted the troops removed as soon as possible. Only an America unified by spiritual purpose, not by force of arms, could, he felt, redeem the sacrifice, in life and limb, of hundreds of thousands of men. Since the African American struggle for equal rights was inflaming the nation's wounds during the bitter Reconstruction years, these political rights would have to remain restricted, though this view, in the immediate postwar years, remained confined to unpublished passages in his manuscripts and to his correspondence.

Yet, as strong and genuine as was Whitman's desire for national unity, he probably would not have been willing to sacrifice abolition and, after the war, African American political rights on its altar had he not accepted the "scientific" racial doctrine of the day, which declared that blacks were, by birth, intellectually inferior to whites. As a child in Brooklyn he had had black friends (though in his public school, the black children were taught separately, on the school's second floor), and there is no evidence that he ever demonstrated, in his *behavior*, any form of prejudice against African Americans. But from early adolescence, when he began to work as a printer's apprentice and reporter at several of the highly politicized Brooklyn newspapers (one of his news items was published when he was twelve, in the Long Island *Patriot*), he would have been steeped in the ideology of the colonization movement, popular throughout the Northeast, especially in Brooklyn and its environs.

Colonization societies, led and financed chiefly by whites, but also including prominent blacks among their leadership, worked for the emigration of free African Americans to the strip of land on the coast of West Africa which, in 1840, achieved independence as

Above

The Battle of Fredericksburg was one of the Civil War's deadliest; on the worst day, December 13, 1862, the total of dead and wounded exceeded 18,000. After reading a name in a newspaper casualty list that he thought might be a garbled form of his brother George's. Whitman, alarmed, set out for Washington, D.C., intending to search the military hospitals for him. Instead, he found George recuperating from a superficial face wound with his unit at Fredericksburg. Shortly thereafter, at a field hospital (probably similar to the one in this undated U.S. Signal Corps photograph), Whitman saw an appalling sight—a cart filled with "a heap of amputated feet, legs, arms, &c."

Below

In the late 1850s, Whitman worked as a volunteer nurse in Manhattan's Broadway Hospital and even assisted the surgeons. With the outbreak of the Civil War, wounded Union soldiers began to fill the beds, and Whitman's ever-present wonder at the nation's human diversity was heightened. Aside from fulfilling a nurse's usual duties, he spent a great deal of time talking with the soldiers, comforting them, bringing them gifts, and writing letters for them. Noted Civil War photographer Mathew Brady made this portrait photograph of Whitman, ca. 1867.

the nation of Liberia. Those advocates who were morally opposed to slavery saw the project as the only realistic answer to America's racial problem, seeing no chance that blacks would ever be allowed to assimilate fully into American society. Others advocated colonization from a far less noble motive—they saw blacks as an alien and potentially destabilizing element in American society. In all probability, the seeds of Whitman's regressive and pessimistic ideas about African American integration were formed during his early exposure to these ideas. In 1858, in the *Brooklyn Daily Times*, Whitman advocated the black colonization cause in phrases that today make us cringe: "Who believes the Whites and Blacks can ever amalgamate in America? Or who wishes it to happen? Nature has set an impassable seal against it. Besides, is not America for the Whites? And is it not better so? As long as Blacks remain here how can they become anything like an independent and heroic race?"[14]

Then, for a brief period, beginning with Abraham Lincoln's second inauguration, Whitman seemed more hopeful than he had ever been about the consequences of black political equality and racial integration. In an 1864 letter, he tells of witnessing the "heterogeneous, novel, and quite inspiriting" sight of freed slaves and black soldiers on the streets of the capital. He also warmly welcomed the increasing visibility of African Americans in Washington society, the most notable signs of which were Frederick Douglass's attendance at Lincoln's inauguration reception and the presence (formerly forbidden) of black spectators in the congressional galleries, where they observed the debates over the Thirteenth Amendment, welcoming its passage with applause and cheers. But with the war's conclusion, Whitman's mood soured. During the congressional Reconstruction debates of 1867, he wrote to friends of his alarm upon seeing raucous crowds of freed slaves, many armed, marching in the streets of Washington for legal and political equality. Such sights confirmed in him the conviction that blacks could not be trusted with political rights in the North or the South, though he expressed this view explicitly only in confidential correspondence and in passages that he excised from essays and articles prior to publication. Intensifying this feeling was a sense of nostalgia for the genteel plantation life (based, of course, on slave labor) he had observed, and for the warm and lively New Orleans men and women he had met while working for several months, in 1848, as a rewriter for the *Daily Crescent*. (Another reason that the charms of New Orleans, and by extension the South, may have remained green in his memory—"O magnet-South! O glistening perfumed South! My South!"—is the homosexual affair that he enjoyed there.)

This is not to say that Whitman would have wanted to maintain slavery in the South merely in order to preserve its genteel traditions. No indication of such a view may be found in his prose, poetry, or correspondence, either published or unpublished. To the contrary, even in the aftermath of his bitterness over Reconstruction, in a piece called "The Late War," placed among the "General Notes" at the end of *Democratic Vistas* (1871), he wrote that "the abolition of Slavery, and the extirpation of the Slaveholding Class [. . .] makes incomparably the longest advance for Radical Democracy, utterly removing its only really dangerous impediment, and insuring its progress in the United States—and thence, of course, over the world." But he *was* troubled by the imposition of military rule on a region of the country that he remembered so fondly, and by its subjection to what he harshly called (and here we encounter one of the most blatantly racist of his published remarks) the "measureless degradation and insult" of "the black domination, but little above the beasts" ("Walt Whitman on the American War," London *Examiner*, 1876). White Southerners, he wrote, were his brothers and sisters—that is, full partners, potentially, in his American dream—whereas African Americans (about whom he wrote with such sympathy, as *slaves*, even as justly angry slaves, despite his view of them as inferior), now that all of them were freed, seemed to him an alien and dangerous presence. In an unpublished manuscript fragment written toward the end of his life, perhaps for a lecture or after-dinner talk, we find the following racially charged statement: "To night I would say one word for that South—the whites. I do not wish to say one word and will not say one word against the blacks—but the blacks can never be to me what the whites are[.] Below all political relations, even the deepest, are still deeper, personal, physiological and emotional ones, the whites are my brothers & I love them."

An indication of the depth of Whitman's ambivalence about America's racial crisis is that he wrote only one poem, after the Lucifer stanzas of "The Sleepers," that focused on race. In this second poem, written near the height of the national debate over Reconstruction and black political rights, he did not reprise the character of Lucifer or attempt to create another dynamic black voice; such an approach would have forced him to reveal the full extent of his racial views, which would have diminished his stature among his progressive friends in America and Britain. Instead, in "Ethiopia Saluting the Colors," written in 1867 and first published in the 1871–72 *Leaves of Grass*, he painted the unthreatening portrait of an old black woman, a former slave. Unlike Lucifer, "Ethiopia" does not verbally express her feelings, she relates only the history of her enslavement, which is confined to three lines (a slaver caught her "as the savage beast is caught," took her from her parents, and brought her to a place across the sea). The brief and sympathetically rendered account (Whitman was not saying that the woman was a beast, but that the slaver treated her as one) is bracketed by the narrative of a Union soldier, who recalls that during his march through the Carolinas as a member of Sherman's victorious army, a black woman ("so ancient hardly human") sitting at the roadside rose and saluted the Union flag. She remained there the entire day as the lengthy troop column passed, wagging her "high-borne turban'd head," rolling her eyes in joy, and offering her courtesies to the troops. The soldier sees her as a "fateful" figure and wonders, rhetorically, if her head wagging means that she is responding to the strange and marvelous scene unfolding before her, or to the equally strange and marvelous scenes she has witnessed in the past. The unarticulated answer is "both." She has witnessed and experienced great suffering and now is overwhelmed by the marvelous instrument of her redemption, Sherman's army, and its iconic emblem, the Union flag.

Whitman, whatever his biases, conscious and unconscious, toward blacks, intended the poem as a sympathetic portrayal of the former slave. His identifying the old woman with Ethiopia, the only African country that had retained its independence in the face of colonial expansion (and that had been featured prominently in recent

Starting from fish=shape Paumanok

Starting from fish=shape Paumanok, where
      I was born,
Well=begotten, and raised by a perfect mother,
After roaming various for many years, lover
      of populous pavements,
Dweller in Mannahatta, the city of ships,
      my city, or on southern savannas,
Or inland and westward, inflating my lungs
      with central Nebraskan air,
Or a soldier camped, or marching bearing
      my knapsack and gun — or a miner
      in California
Or rude in my home in Kanuck woods,
      or a hunter, my drink from the spring,
      my diet meat,
Or withdrawn to meditate in some deep recess,
Far from the clank of crowds, my ecstasy
      passing, rapt and happy,
Aware of the fresh free=giver the flowing Missouri,
      aware of mighty Niagara,
Aware of the buffalo herds the grazing
      the plains, the hirsute and strong=breasted bull,
Of earth, rocks, Fifth Month flowers experienced —
      stars, rain, snow, my amaze,
Having studied the mocking=bird's tones, and the
      mountain hawk,
And heard at dusk the hermit thrush from the
      swamp=cedar,
Solitary, singing in the west, I strike up for a
      new world.

This is the first page of the famous copy of the 1860–61 edition that Whitman thoroughly revised in his own hand during the Civil War years and afterwards, as he prepared the text of what would become his 1867 [i.e., 1868] edition of *Leaves of Grass*. Bound in blue paper wrappers, it has become known as the "Blue Book." This volume was also the cause of Whitman's dismissal from his clerkship in the Bureau of Indian Affairs, when Secretary of the Interior James Harlan found it in Whitman's desk in May 1865. Harlan, who had resolved to dismiss employees showing poor "moral character," was so horrified and angered by what he read that he fired Whitman on the spot.

news accounts for asserting itself against the British),[15] is a recognition of a rich tradition of African political independence (as others have noted, "high-borne" is intended to recall "high-born"),[16] and an expression of hope that perhaps the dignity enshrined in Ethiopian sovereignty might be won by African Americans. ("So ancient hardly human" means that Ethiopia's antiquity, i.e., the antiquity of the people she personifies, gives her a mythic quality that almost transcends humanity.) The colors that the ancient former slave salutes are not only those of the Union flag, but, in a foreshadowing of African Americans reclaiming their birthright of human dignity, the "yellow, red and green" of her turban—the colors of the Ethiopian flag. But this was as far as Whitman was prepared to venture. How blacks were to win America's acknowledgment of their human dignity without being able to vote and exercise their political will is a question that he does not address. It would have been instructive for Whitman to imagine what Lucifer would have had to say about the charms of Southern life, and how his human (much less civil) rights were to be protected without the presence of federal troops in Whitman's "glistening perfumed South."

As in his poetry, so in his published prose: Whitman almost entirely avoids a serious engagement with America's postwar racial problem. The issue is virtually ignored even in *Democratic Vistas* (1871), a defense of American society and its political institutions (though America's faults, racial discrimination *not* among them, are frankly admitted), and a look forward to the glories that American democracy may yet achieve. The book is a reworking and expansion of three essays from the late 1860s (two of which appeared in *Galaxy* magazine). The writing of at least one of the essays had been prompted by Thomas Carlyle's essay "Shooting Niagara: And After?" (1867), in which Carlyle had attacked, among other newfangled notions, Britain's Reform movement and American-style democracy. The latter, he said, had infected Britain to such a shocking extent that substantial numbers of MPs had foolishly advocated abolishing property ownership as a suffrage requirement. But Carlyle saved his most savage ridicule for what he saw as American democracy's most recent manifestation of lunacy, the Civil War, which he characterized as an extreme instance of

"Swarmery," that is, the mindless swarming of men around whatever cause piques their easily misled fancies. He saw the war as a predictable, if particularly disastrous and horrific, consequence of democracy's fatal tendency toward sentimental adventurism, in which armies "of excellent White Men, full of gifts and faculties, have torn and slashed one another into horrid death, in a temporary humour, which will leave centuries of remembrance fierce enough; and three million absurd Blacks, men and brothers (of a sort) are completely 'emancipated': launched into the career of improvement—likely to be 'improved off the face of the earth' in a generation or two!"[17]

Though Carlyle devoted most of "Shooting Niagara" to speculation about the kinds of service to which the English aristocracy might devote itself in order to improve Britain and her empire (as a bulwark against the encroachments of democracy), Whitman's fighting spirit was aroused by Carlyle's "Feudal" arguments against American democracy, and he responded to these by surveying his country's cultural achievements, mores, and social and political institutions, both as they existed and as he hoped they would develop in coming generations. He constructed his counterarguments with assuredness and confidence, explaining why it was a good thing that America's press was freer to express its views and that its political and judicial institutions were more representative than their British and European counterparts. Though he readily admitted that he had seen little in American literature that pleased him, he felt confident that the country would soon produce a pioneering, uniquely American form of literary expression, no doubt thinking of the invigorating influence of his own work. But despite his confident tone in treating these important political and cultural subjects, he is circumspect to the point of silence regarding Carlyle's chief piece of "evidence" in his argument against American democracy—that the abolition of slavery resulted only in the wasted lives "of excellent Whte Men" and the impossible task of assimilating blacks into American society. Whitman's reticence speaks eloquently about his discomfort with the issue, since he knows that he cannot respond truthfully without revealing his own deep reservations about the role that blacks might play in postwar America.

Two oblique references to African Americans, in *Democratic Vistas* (1871), substantiate this interpretation. Early in the book, Whitman refers to the "priceless value" of "general suffrage," but he later retreats from this unqualified advocacy to the concession that he "will not gloss over the appaling [*sic*] dangers of universal suffrage." The latter remark, in the context of a response to Carlyle, can only be taken as an admission that, at the very least, Whitman thought it probable that blacks were politically unassimilable in white society, a view that, as we saw, he had earlier expressed explicitly. In a footnote, he goes so far as to admit that he has occasionally been provoked into a reaction similar to Carlyle's, though he does not, as he did in 1858, give free reign to his feelings on the subject. And in the *Galaxy* article from which one of the *Democratic Vistas* essays was adapted, Whitman, in two places, mocks Carlyle's demeaning caricatures of blacks, but by heightening the caricature in phrases that are too exuberant to have been written by someone who did not share Carlyle's bias.[18] In reworking the *Galaxy* essays into the text that became *Democratic Vistas*, Whitman probably realized that these phrases revealed too much of his true racial views, saw that they might jeopardize his legacy as an avatar of brotherhood, and therefore omitted the mocking passages from the book.

Perhaps the most troubling of Whitman's statements on race is an unpublished passage about black suffrage that appears in his manuscript for an 1874 compilation, "A Christmas Garland, in Prose and Verse," that was published in New York's *Daily Graphic*: "As if we had not strained the voting and digestive caliber of American Democracy to the utmost for the last fifty years with the millions of ignorant foreigners, we have now infused a powerful percentage of blacks, with about as much intellect and caliber (in the mass) as so many baboons. But we stood the former trial—solved it—and, though this is much harder, will, I doubt not, triumphantly solve this." Such ugliness is, inevitably, shocking and dispiriting to those for whom Whitman's expansive, affectionate presence emanates from the leaves of his open book, spanning a gulf of 150 years in the time it takes to read such lines as those that conclude "Song of Myself":

I bequeath myself to the dirt to grow from the grass I love,
If you want me again look for me under your bootsoles.

You will hardly know who I am or what I mean,
But I shall be good health to you nevertheless,
And filter and fibre your blood.

Failing to fetch me at first keep encouraged,
Missing me one place search another,
I stop some where waiting for you.

Poetry such as this can only intensify our sense of betrayal at
Whitman's unpublished *Daily Graphic* passage (and others of the
same ilk), especially since his racism finds no expression in *Leaves*,
as if he knew that such views were unworthy of his great poem—
what might be considered his "better" self.[19]

Less generously, one might surmise that he was afraid to
express his racial views in *Leaves*, or in the prose that he published in
book form, because it would damage his public image as a wise and
gentle sage—"the good gray poet"—and appall his progressive friends
and supporters (which may have been the source of his estrangement
from his friend William D. O'Connor in the 1870s). But even if we grant
that Whitman saw *Leaves of Grass* as the expression of all that was best
in him, and therefore left out of it all that was worst, it is only natural
that we should ask, why could he not find in his "best" even a single
poem that envisioned black camerados and sisters tramping the perpetual journey with him, helping to fulfill the sacred destiny of the country
he loved so much? The question, of course, is unanswerable, and as
Whitman might have said, "I answer the unanswerable with a paradox,"
of which he provided many, but few as apt as his most famous: "Do I
contradict myself? Very well then, I contradict myself." Or, as George
Orwell, another master of paradox, and a deflator of pretensions to
boot, might have noted, with a small, hard smile: "We are all One, but
some are more One than others."

Notes

1. The poems quoted here appear in their original versions. Since those that first appeared in the 1855 edition were untitled, the titles under which they later became best known have been supplied for ease of identification: "Song of Myself," "A Song for Occupations," "To Think of Time," and "The Sleepers."

2. The similarity of content and tone between Whitman and Nietzsche is often uncanny, though Nietzsche did not read Whitman; the first German translation of *Leaves of Grass* appeared only in 1907, and *Thus Spake Zarathustra* was published in 1883. One might appeal for an explanation to the mid- and late-century zeitgeist, probably engendered by German Romanticism, illustrated also in Oscar Wilde's frequent use of the paradoxical epigram, though his examples of the form are, essentially, witty quips intended to shock the reader and to display his own cleverness, rather than, like Whitman's and, arguably, Nietzsche's paradoxes, serious attempts to awaken and transform.

3. Whitman made frequent use of ellipses, employing from two to five dots. In order to distinguish between these and the ellipses inserted by the present writer, the latter have been placed in brackets.

4. Other such passages include: "This minute that comes to me over the past decillions, / There is no better than it and now" ("Song of Myself"); "there is something that comes home to one now and perpetually" ("A Song for Occupations"); "wonders that fill each minute of time forever" ("A Song for Occupations").

5. In *Democratic Vistas* (1871), Whitman declares that the two principles on which true democracy rests are "the principle of the average" and "individuality," which he also calls "identity-personalism." All of humanity's important cultural advances, he says, may be reduced "to the consideration of a single self, a man, a woman." Even in the political or metaphysical realms, "sooner or later we come down to one single, solitary soul." Whitman then tries to give the reader a sense of what it feels like to be a true individual, an account that harmonizes with the "Me myself" passage in "Song of Myself": "a consciousness, a thought that rises, independent, lifted out from all else, calm, like the stars, shining eternal. This is the thought of identity— yours for you, whoever you are, as mine for me. Miracle of miracles, beyond statement, most spiritual and vaguest of earth's dreams, yet hardest basic fact, and only entrance to all facts. In such devout hours, in the midst of the significant wonders of heaven and earth (significant only because of the Me in the center), creeds, conventions, fall away and become of no account before this simple idea. Under the luminousness of real vision it alone takes possession, takes value. Like the shadowy dwarf in the fable, once liberated and looked upon, it expands over the whole earth, and spreads to the roof of heaven."

6. "Men and women perceive the beauty well enough . . probably as well as he"; "Men and women and the earth and all upon it are simply to be taken as they are"; "Liberty takes the adherence of heroes wherever men and women exist"; "the true taste of the women and men you pass or have to do with in youth or middle age"; "the new breed of poets be interpreters of men and women" (all from the preface to the 1855 edition).

7. Other instances, all from "Song of Myself," include: "I wish I could translate the hints about the dead young men and women"; "[the poet is] no stander above men and women or apart from them"; "Wherever he goes men and women accept and desire him."

8. Though Whitman describes himself as the would-be impregnator of every "warm-blooded" American woman, his statement that he will "graft the grafts of the best-

beloved of me and of America" on them shows that he is speaking metaphorically and that what he prophesies or hopes for is that the men and women he has inspired with his "love-spendings" (i.e., his spiritual essence) will mate with each other and thereby produce "perfect men and women."

9. Modern readers may, however, be surprised to find that *Leaves of Grass* contains evidence of Whitman's support for the anti-masturbation medical theories of his time: "the sick-gray faces of onanists" ("The Sleepers").

10. One should not forget, however, that even the 1855 *Leaves of Grass* contains evidence of Whitman's homosexuality. In "Song of Myself," he begins a lengthy metaphor in which he imagines that the earth is an extension of his body ("If I worship any particular thing it shall be some of the spread of my body"), but as the descriptions comprising this metaphorized male body are listed, it becomes increasingly clear that the body is his lover's:

> Mixed tussled hay of head and beard and brawn it
>   shall be you,
> Trickling sap of maple, fibre of manly wheat, it
>   shall be you;
> . . . You sweaty brooks and dews it shall be you,
> Winds whose soft-tickling genitals rub against me
>   it shall be you,
> Broad muscular fields, branches of liveoak, loving
>   lounger in my winding paths, it shall be you,
> Hands I have taken, face I have kissed, mortal I
>   have ever touched, it shall be you.

11. Complementing the evidence of this excision is the bibliographical and textual analysis of Fredson Bowers, first published in his "Whitman's Manuscripts for the Original 'Calamus' Poems," *Studies in Bibliography: Papers of the Bibliographical Society of the University of Virginia*, vol. 6 (1954): 257–65, and, with several emendations, in his Introduction to *Whitman's Manuscripts: Leaves of Grass (1860); A Parallel Text. Edited with Notes and Introduction by*

Fredson Bowers (Chicago: University of Chicago Press, 1955). Bowers analyzed a twelve-poem notebook (housed in the University of Virginia Library's Clifton Waller Barrett Collection) that Whitman titled "Live Oak, with Moss," demonstrating that the poem cycle told the story of a homosexual affair. Bowers further showed how Whitman revised these twelve poems and disrupted their sequence when he incorporated them into the larger poem cluster that was titled "Calamus."

12. The summary of Whitman's racial views presented here is adapted largely, though with occasional divergences in emphasis and interpretation, from Ed Folsom's "Lucifer and Ethiopia: Whitman, Race, and Poetics Before the Civil War and After," *A Historical Guide to Walt Whitman*, ed. David S. Reynolds (New York: Oxford University Press, 2000), 45–95.

13. Ibid., 49.

14. Ibid., 76.

15. See ibid., 59–64, for a summary of the events that brought Ethiopia prominently into America's consciousness in 1867 and 1868.

16. Ibid., 82.

17. Ibid., 77–78.

18. In the latter of these, he says that Carlyle's "vituperative cat-squalling" about "the Niagara leap" and "swarmery" is more extreme than anything he has encountered at a Tennessee revival meeting "or Bedlam let loose in crowded, colored Carolina bush-meeting," quoted, in part, ibid., 79.

19. To his credit, he retained the incendiary "Lucifer" poem in the 1867 and 1871–72 editions, even as his disenchantment with the campaign for black political rights was growing.

46

(follow copy, italics and all, line for line) 2

Rich A Child's Reminiscence.

Pre=verse.

Out of the rocked cradle,
Out of the mocking=bird's throat, the
    musical shuttle,
Out of the boy's mother's womb, and from
    the nipples of her breasts,
Out of the Ninth-Month midnight,
Over the sterile sea=sands, and the fields
    beyond, where the child, leaving his
    bed, wandered alone, bare=headed,
    bare=foot,
Down from the showered halo and the
    moonbeams,
Up from the mystic play of shadows
    twining and twisting as if they
    were alive,
Out from the patches of briars and
    blackberries,
From the memories of the bird that
    chanted to me
From your memories, sad brother — from
    the fitful risings and fallings I
    heard,

"A Child's Reminiscence," which first appeared in the New York
Saturday Press of December 24, 1859, was later published, in
somewhat revised form, in the 1860–61 edition of *Leaves of Grass* as
"A Word Out of the Sea." In the 1871–72 edition, it received the
new first line from which its best-known title, "Out of the Cradle
Endlessly Rocking," is derived, as shown in this manuscript.

Checklist of the Exhibition

Except where otherwise indicated, materials are from the Henry W. and Albert A. Berg Collection of English and American Literature. Items illustrated in this publication are indicated by an asterisk (*); the number of the page on which the illustration appears is given in brackets at the end of the entry.

INTRODUCTION

Unknown photographer. Walt Whitman Birthplace, West Hills, Huntington, Long Island, 1902; printed ca. 1993

N. S. Packard, artist. Pen-and-ink drawing of Walt Whitman's House, Mickle Street, Camden, New Jersey, signed, n.d.

Unknown photographer. Portrait photograph of Walt Whitman, ca. 1880

*[Gabriel Harrison?], photographer. Portrait daguerreotype of Walt Whitman, 1853 or 1854. *Rare Books Division, Oscar Lion Collection* [cover; frontispiece]

Walt Whitman. "Song of Myself." Autograph prose notes and verse drafts, 1854 or 1855, 24 p. *Rare Books Division, Oscar Lion Collection*

Walt Whitman. *Leaves of Grass*, with 11 Whitman autograph "Preface" booklets affixed to and laid-in between blank leaves at front and back of volume. Brooklyn, N.Y.: [Andrew and James Rome for Walt Whitman], 1855 (2nd issue). *Rare Books Division, Oscar Lion Collection*

THE 1855 EDITION

*Walt Whitman. *Leaves of Grass*. Brooklyn, N.Y.: [Andrew and James Rome for Walt Whitman]; London: [Andrew and James Rome for Walt Whitman and] William Horsell, 1855 (2nd issue) [page 28]

*Walt Whitman. *Leaves of Grass*. Brooklyn, N.Y.: [Andrew and James Rome for Walt Whitman], 1855 (1st issue, 2nd state). *Provenance: Owen D. Young* [page 10]

Walt Whitman. *Leaves of Grass*. Brooklyn, N.Y.: [Andrew and James Rome for Walt Whitman], 1855 (1st issue, 2nd state). *Provenance: W.T.H. Howe*

Walt Whitman. *Leaves of Grass*. Brooklyn, N.Y.: [Andrew and James Rome for Walt Whitman], 1855 (1st issue, 2nd state) (2 copies)

Walt Whitman. *Leaves of Grass*. Brooklyn, N.Y.: [Andrew and James Rome for Walt Whitman], 1855 (1st issue). *Provenance: Owen D. Young*

THE 1856 EDITION

*Unknown photographer. Portrait photograph of Ralph Waldo Emerson, ca. 1855 [page 17]

*Walt Whitman. "Emerson, An Appreciation." Autograph manuscript, ca. 1854, 2 p. [page 17]

Walt Whitman. *Leaves of Grass*. Brooklyn, N.Y.: [Walt Whitman, sold by Fowler and Wells], 1856 (3 copies)

James Joyce. *Ulysses*. Paris: Shakespeare and Company, 1922. Copy 474 of 1,000

Gisèle Freund, photographer. James Joyce and Sylvia Beach in doorway of Shakespeare and Company bookshop, Paris, 1921. *Provenance: Sylvia Beach*

*Unknown photographer. Stereoscopic view of a Brooklyn ferry, ca. 1870. *Miriam and Ira D. Wallach Division of Art, Prints and Photographs, Photography Collection, Robert Dennis Collection of Stereoscopic Views* [page 13]

*Walt Whitman. "Crossing Brooklyn Ferry." Proof copy, with Whitman's manuscript corrections, 1881; autograph emendations ca. 1888; [18] p. [page 13]

THE 1860–61 EDITION AND THE CIVIL WAR

*Walt Whitman. *Leaves of Grass*. Boston: Thayer and Eldridge, 1860–61 (1st issue, 1st state) (3 copies) [pages 27, 28]

Walt Whitman. *Leaves of Grass*. Boston: Thayer and Eldridge, 1860–61 (1st issue, 2nd state, buff tinting of portrait) (2 copies)

*Walt Whitman. "A Child's Reminiscence." Autograph manuscript, ca. 1859, 15 p. [page 46]

Gurney and Son, photographer. Portrait photograph of Walt Whitman, 1872, signed and dated by Whitman; later inserted in: [Whitman Family Record manuscript], ca. 1850, 1860

Unknown photographer. Portrait photograph of Abraham Lincoln, 1864; letterpress half-tone reproduction, 1891. *Miriam and Ira D. Wallach Division of Art, Prints and Photographs, Photography Collection*

*Walt Whitman. "I Saw in Louisiana a Live-Oak Growing." Autograph draft fragment, [1857–59?], 1 p. [page 30]

[Alexander Gardner?], photographer. Portrait photograph of Walt Whitman, [1864]

Unknown photographer. "The Sixth Maine Infantry on Parade After Fredericksburg," [1862]. From "The Pageant of America" Collection, vol. 7. *Miriam and Ira D. Wallach Division of Art, Prints and Photographs, Photography Collection*

Levin Corbin, photographer. "Antietam Field, View West Side Hagerstown," [1862]. From "The Pageant of America" Collection, vol. 7. *Miriam and Ira D. Wallach Division of Art, Prints and Photographs, Photography Collection*

*Unknown photographer, United States Signal Corps. "Wounded Soldiers in Hospital," n.d. From "The Pageant of America" Collection, vol. 7. *Miriam and Ira D. Wallach Division of Art, Prints and Photographs, Photography Collection* [page 35]

Walt Whitman. *Drum-Taps*. New York: [Peter Eckler], 1865 (1st issue) (3 copies)

Walt Whitman. *Leaves of Grass*. With Wood-Engravings by Boyd Hanna. Mount Vernon, N.Y.: Peter Pauper Press, [1950]. One of 1,100 copies

Walt Whitman. Autograph letter, signed, to Louisa Van Velsor Whitman, Washington, [D.C.], June 30, 1863, 8 p.

*Mathew Brady, photographer. Portrait photograph of Walt Whitman, ca. 1867 [page 35]

Unknown photographer. "Knickerbockers Nine," 1864. *George Arents Collection, Goulston Collection*

Walt Whitman. *Drum-Taps*, with Whitman's autograph emendations. Washington, D.C. [i.e., New York: J. S. Redfield], 1871 (2nd issue); autograph emendations ca. 1880

Unknown photographer. Stereoscopic portrait photograph of Abraham Lincoln, [1865]. From "The Pageant of America" Collection, vol. 7: "In Defense of Liberty" (unpublished photographs). *Miriam and Ira D. Wallach Division of Art, Prints and Photographs, Photography Collection*

Walt Whitman. *Sequel to Drum-Taps (Since the Preceding Came from the Press): When Lilacs Last in the Door-Yard Bloom'd. And Other Pieces*. Washington, [D.C.]: [J. S. Redfield], 1865–66

Walt Whitman. *Memories of President Lincoln*, with Whitman's autograph emendations. Washington, D.C. [i.e., New York]: J. S. Redfield, 1871 [i.e., 1870]; autograph emendations ca. 1875

*Walt Whitman. *Leaves of Grass*, with autograph emendations and with manuscript pages affixed to several leaves of text [the "Blue Book"]. Boston: Thayer and Eldridge, 1860–61 (2nd issue). *Rare Books Division, Oscar Lion Collection* [page 39]

THE 1867 EDITION

Walt Whitman. *Leaves of Grass*. New York: [William E. Chapin], 1867 [i.e., 1868] (1st issue)

Walt Whitman. Leaves removed, and emended in Whitman's hand, from *Leaves of Grass* and *Drum-Taps*. New York: [William E. Chapin], 1867 [i.e., 1868] for *Leaves of Grass* (2 copies); New York: [Peter Eckler], 1865 for *Drum-Taps*

PASSAGE TO INDIA

Unknown photographer. Portrait photograph of Walt Whitman, [Brooklyn], ca. 1870–71

Frank Pearsall, photographer. Portrait photograph of Walt Whitman, [Brooklyn, 1872]. *Rare Books Division, Oscar Lion Collection*

Walt Whitman. "The Spinal Idea." Autograph manuscript in notebook for the book *Passage to India*, [1869], 13 p. *Rare Books Division, Oscar Lion Collection*

*Walt Whitman. *Passage to India*. Autograph manuscript, [1869], 23 p., numbered 1–21. *Rare Books Division, Oscar Lion Collection* [page 18]

Andrew J. Russell, photographer. "Valley of the Great Laramie." In: *The Great West Illustrated in a Series of Photographic Views of the Continent Taken Along the Line of the Union Pacific Railroad . . .* (New York, 1869). *Miriam and Ira D. Wallach Division of Art, Prints and Photographs, Photography Collection*

THE 1871–72 [I.E., 1870] EDITION

Frank Pearsall, photographer. Portrait photograph of Walt Whitman, [Brooklyn, 1872]

Walt Whitman. *Leaves of Grass*. Washington, D.C.: J. S. Redfield, 1871–72 [i.e., 1870]

TWO RIVULETS AND THE 1876 EDITION

Walt Whitman. Two Rivulets, Including *Democratic Vistas, Centennial Songs, and Passage to India*. Author's Edition. Camden, N.J., 1876

Walt Whitman. "The Ox Tamer." Autograph manuscript, [1875?], 1 p.

Walt Whitman. "As a Strong Bird on Pinions Free." Autograph manuscript, [1875?], 13 leaves

Walt Whitman. "Go Said My Soul." Four autograph drafts, [1876?], 1 p.

THE 1881–82 EDITION

Napoleon Sarony, photographer. Portrait photograph of Walt Whitman, 37 Union Square, New York, 1879

William D. O'Connor. Autograph letter, signed, to John Burroughs, Washington, D.C., May 3, 1882, 12 p. (3 sheets folded into 6 leaves)

Walt Whitman/Richard Maurice Bucke. "Analysis of Leaves of Grass." Autograph draft, [1883], 191 p.

Walt Whitman. *Leaves of Grass*. Boston: James R. Osgood and Co., 1881–82 (1st state)

Walt Whitman. *Leaves of Grass*. Boston: James R. Osgood and Co., 1881–82

Walt Whitman. *Leaves of Grass*. Philadelphia: [Sherman & Co.] for Rees Welsh & Co., 1882

FINAL POEMS AND THE 1891–92 EDITION

Walt Whitman. *Good-Bye My Fancy: 2d Annex to Leaves of Grass*. Philadelphia: David McKay, 1891. *Provenance: Alfred, Lord Tennyson*

Walt Whitman. *Leaves of Grass, Including Sands at Seventy . . . 1st Annex, Good-Bye My Fancy . . . 2d Annex, A Backward Glance O'er Travel'd Roads, and Portrait from Life*. Philadelphia: David McKay, 1891–92

INFLUENCE

Edward Weston, photographer. Portrait photograph of D. H. Lawrence, ca. 1925?

D. H. Lawrence. *Studies in Classic American Literature*. New York: Thomas Seltzer, 1923

John Cohen, photographer. Photograph of Jack Kerouac, 1959

Jack Kerouac. *On the Road*. Typescript with black crayon and pencil emendations, ca. 1951, 297 p.; with 12-page autograph manuscript in pencil on verso of pp. 46–35. *Berg Collection, Jack Kerouac Archive*

Ann Charters, photographer. Photograph of Allen Ginsberg reading poetry, ca. 1970?

Allen Ginsberg. *Howl and Other Poems*. Introduction by William Carlos Williams, with Ginsberg's autograph annotations. San Francisco: The City Lights Pocket Bookshop, 1956 (1st printing)

James Johnston, photographer. Portrait photograph of Walt Whitman, [Philadelphia], 1890

CONCLUSION

Unknown photographer. Portrait photograph of Walt Whitman, May 1882

E. Gutekunst, photographer. Portrait photo-engraving (phototype) of Walt Whitman, Philadelphia, 1887

Walt Whitman. Lock of hair, October 29, 1891, and sheet fom *Boston Evening*, May 7, 1891

Selected Bibliography

COLLECTIONS AND EDITIONS OF WHITMAN'S WRITINGS

Walt Whitman's Leaves of Grass. The First (1855) Edition. Edited and with an introduction by Malcolm Cowley. New York: Viking Press, 1959.

Walt Whitman's Leaves of Grass. Afterword by David S. Reynolds. New York: Oxford University Press, 2005 [150th anniversary facsimile of the 1855 edition].

"Leaves of Grass": A Textual Variorum of the Printed Poems. Edited by Sculley Bradley, et al. 3 vols. New York: New York University Press, 1980.

Leaves of Grass and Other Writings. Edited by Michael Moon. New York: W. W. Norton, 2002.

Complete Poetry and Collected Prose. Edited by Justin Kaplan. New York: Library of America, 1982.

The Correspondence. Edited by Edwin Haviland Miller. 6 vols. New York: New York University Press, 1961–77.

Daybooks and Notebooks. Edited by William H. White. 3 vols. New York: New York University Press, 1978.

Notebooks and Unpublished Prose Manuscripts: Walt Whitman. Edited by Edward F. Grier. 6 vols. New York: New York University Press, 1984.

Walt Whitman: The Journalism. Edited by Herbert Bergman et al. New York: Peter Lang, 1998.

BIOGRAPHICAL AND CRITICAL WORKS

Fone, Byrne. *Masculine Landscapes: Walt Whitman and the Homoerotic Text*. Carbondale: Southern Illinois University Press, 1992.

Killingsworth, M. *Whitman's Poetry of the Body: Sexuality, Politics, and the Text*. Chapel Hill: University of North Carolina Press, 1989.

Loving, Jerome. *Walt Whitman: The Song of Himself*. Berkeley: University of California Press, 1999.

Myerson, Joel. *Walt Whitman: A Descriptive Bibliography*. "Pittsburgh Studies in Bibliography." Pittsburgh: University of Pittsburgh Press, 1993. The definitive bibliography.

Price, Kenneth M. *Whitman and Tradition: The Poet in His Century*. New Haven: Yale University Press, 1990.

Reynolds, David S. *Walt Whitman's America: A Cultural Biography*. New York: Vintage, 1996.

Reynolds, David S., ed. *A Historical Guide to Walt Whitman*. New York: Oxford University Press, 2000.

Shively, Charles, ed. *Calamus Lovers: Walt Whitman's Working-class Camerados*. San Francisco: Gay Sunshine, 1987.

Zweig, Paul. *Walt Whitman: The Making of the Poet*. New York: Basic Books, 1984.

Many persons must be thanked for their contributions to this exhibition and catalogue, first and foremost, H. George Fletcher, Brooke Russell Astor Director for Special Collections and the administrator and guiding spirit of The New York Public Library's Exhibitions Program, for his overall leadership and support, and for communicating throughout the Library the importance of mounting this exhibition. Karen Van Westering, Manager of the Publications Program, wisely conceived the plan for the exhibition catalogue, and ably supervised its editing, production, and design: Barbara Bergeron, Editor, used her keen and vigilant eye to discover and correct grammatical sins and stylistic infelicities, while maintaining sympathy for authorial intentions; Jennifer Woolf, Associate Editor, gathered the digital images for the catalogue's illustrations; and Catherine Harvey designed the catalogue.

The exhibition itself could not have been mounted without the energetic management and supervision of Susan Rabbiner, Manager of the Exhibitions Program, whose fine staff undertook all aspects of the exhibition's preparation and installation: Jeanne Bornstein, Research Coordinator, and Meg Maher, Assistant Research Coordinator, who shepherded staff efforts in the preparation of text for Registrar Office documentation, labels, and flyer; Jean Mihich, Registrar, and Caryn Gedell, Associate Registrar, who carefully maintained the documentation and recorded the disposition of exhibition materials during the lengthy preparation period; Myriam De Arteni, Exhibitions Conservator, and her staff, for their meticulous and sensitive work on the exhibition's rare books, manuscripts, and photographs; and Russell Drisch, Installation Coordinator and Designer, and his staff, especially Patrick Day, for creatively accommodating the exhibition to the gallery cases and walls, allowing a wide variety of materials to be displayed in a manner that sustains the exhibition's narrative, as well as for their custom fabrication of display mounts and for framing manuscripts and photographs. The imagination and hard work of Suzanne Doig, of the Library's Graphics Office, resulted in a vivid design, evocative of Whitman's spirit, for the exhibition poster, flyer, and catalogue cover. Instructional programs related to the exhibition, including lectures by the Curator, were carefully conceived and coordinated by Philip Yockey, Manager of Public Instruction, and his assistant Amy Azzarito, to whom we are indebted. For an evening of stellar, Whitmanian proportions, featuring a reading and talk by the literary critic Harold Bloom, we thank Paul Holdengräber, Director of Public Programs for The Research Libraries.

The great majority of items displayed in the exhibition are from the Berg Collection, but the exhibition would have been much the poorer absent the materials graciously made available by the Rare Books Division's Michael Inman; by Stephen Pinson, Curator of the Photography Collection, Miriam and Ira D. Wallach Division of Art, Prints and Photographs, and his most helpful assistant David Lowe, who gave generously of his time in order to present a rich selection of appropriate photographs; and by Virginia Bartow, Curator of the George Arents Collection, whose knowledge enabled her to make the perfect suggestion for an Arents contribution. The Rare Books Division is the home of the Oscar Lion Collection of Walt Whitman, and among its treasures are a unique print of a daguerreotype of Whitman, dating from 1854–55 (reproduced to dramatic effect on the cover of this volume); a small notebook containing the earliest known draft of and notes for the poem that was later titled "Song of Myself"; Whitman's own copy of the 1855 edition, with eleven prefaces written from 1855 to 1870, unpublished in his lifetime, affixed or laid-in the volume; and his copy of the 1860–61 edition, wrapped in blue paper (i.e., the famous "Blue Book"), which he used as a proof copy for the preparation of the text that would become the 1867 edition. The Photography Collection provided photographs of Abraham Lincoln, of a Civil War hospital and other Civil War scenes, of the Wyoming mountains and plains (of which Whitman sang without having visited them), and of a Brooklyn ferry upon which Whitman might have traveled. To the Arents Collection we are indebted for an 1864 photograph of the New York baseball team the "Knickerbockers Nine," a visual complement to Whitman's often expressed love of "the American game," as he, apparently, was the first to call it.